Seaman statue at San Pedro's Ports O'Call being admired by Thorsten Korth.

SOUTHERN CALIFORNIA'S SEA COAST

THEN & NOW

Neptune's statue in Palos Verdes. Roman god of the sea, identified with the Greek Poseidon (399 BC).

SOUTHERN CALIFORNIA'S SEACOAST

THEN & NOW

By HOWARD GREGORY

HOWARD GREGORY ASSOCIATES,   REDONDO BEACH, CALIFORNIA

*Father Junipero Serra (1713–1784) statue at Ventura. He founded
Mission San Diego on July 16, 1769. Between 1770 and 1782 he
founded eight additional missions ending with San Buenaventura in
1782. He was president of the lower California missions and was
known as the Apostle of California.*

THANKS

Juan Rodriguez Cabrillo (died in the vicinity of the Santa Barbara Channel Jan. 3, 1543) statue at Cabrillo Beach in San Pedro. A Portuguese navigator in the Spanish service. He discovered the Southern California seacoast in 1542.

"Where did you get the pictures?" is the first thing that most people say when they see the beautiful old photographs.

With sincere gratitude I would like to acknowledge the assistance received from many people up and down the California seacoast. I want to especially thank John McGehee (540 23rd Street, Manhattan Beach, CA 90266) who is a high school teacher in Palos Verdes. All of the old photos of Manhattan Beach, Hermosa Beach, Redondo Beach and Palos Verdes are from John's collection. John's avocation is making beautiful, matted sepia toned pictures which he sells commercially in the Los Angeles South Bay area.

I would like to also thank Diane Nassir of the University of California at Santa Barbara Library; Peter L. Bandurroga of the Ventura Historical Museum; The Strickfaden Collection (Santa Monica History); The Santa Monica Library; Julia Brown of the California Historical Society/Title Insurance and Trust Co. (Los Angeles) collection of Historical Photographs; the Venice Camera Exchange; Edward Hauck — Curator, Los Angeles Maritime Museum; Department of Small Craft Harbors — County of Los Angeles at Marina del Rey; the Boschetto Studio of El Segundo; the El Segundo Library; the Northrop News; the Long Beach Public Library; the Newport Beach Historical Society; BC Photography/BC Space of Laguna Beach; the Laguna Beach Chamber of Commerce and the Laguna Beach Historical Society; Mrs. Elizabeth N. Shor of the Scripps Institution of Oceanography (now part of the University of California, San Diego) of La Jolla; the San Diego Historical Society/Title Insurance and Trust Historical Collection and Bob Urhausen of the Goodyear Airship Operations.

A special appreciation is given to all the people who were gracious enough to consent to pose in the "NOW" photos; their names are listed with the pictures. All of the "NOW" photos were taken by the author, Howard Gregory.

Published by
HOWARD GREGORY ASSOCIATES
640 The Village #209
Redondo Beach, California 90277

International Standard Book Number (ISBN) 0-9607086-0-X (Softbound Edition)
International Standard Book Number (ISBN) 0-9607086-1-8 (Hardcover Edition)
Library of Congress Catalog Card Number 81-90472

First Printing 1982
Second Printing 1983

THIS BOOK IS AVAILABLE FROM YOUR LOCAL BOOKSTORE.
THE BOOK IS ALSO AVAILABLE BY MAIL ORDER FROM:

HOWARD GREGORY
640 THE VILLAGE #209
REDONDO BEACH, CALIFORNIA 90277

Other books by Howard Gregory: "The Falcon's Disciples" and a revised larger edition: "Parachuting's Unforgettable Jumps"

PRINTED IN THE UNITED STATES OF AMERICA
BY Delta Lithograph • Van Nuys, CA

CONTENTS

Neptune's statue in Palos Verdes. Roman god of the sea, identified with the Greek Poseidon (399 BC).

COVER: Hermosa Pier in 1905 from the John McGehee Collection. Hermosa Pier today with Denise Vile and Jocelyne Smith. Cover art work by Meek Communications, Hermosa Beach.

HISTORIC PHOTO CREDITS: U.C. Santa Barbara Library (9–15); Ventura Historical Museum (16–19); The Strickfadden Collection (20, 23-29, 31-34, 36-38); California Historical Society at Los Angeles (21, 22, 26, 30, 35); Santa Monica Library (23, 29, 36-38); Venice Camera Exchange (39-48); Dept. of Small Craft Harbors County of Los Angeles (49-52); Boshetto Studio (53, 54); Northrop News (55, 56); Murphy Studio (57, 58); John McGehee Collections (59-102); Los Angeles Maritime Museum (103-121, 134, 135, 137, 138); Long Beach Public Library (124-133); Newport Beach Historical Society (139, 140); BC Photography/BC Space (143, 144, 151); Laguna Beach Chamber of Commerce (141, 142, 145-150); Scripps Institution of Oceanography (152-156); San Diego Historical Society (157-165); Goodyear Airship Operations (167).

PREFACE

THEN & NOW photographs tell fascinating stories in the blink of an eye. To see what was once upon a time: alive, vibrant, active people and places as they were and suddenly it's a century later. The contrast between the two photographs conjures instantaneous time travel.

Researching the old photographs for this book in Historical Societies; Museums; Chambers of Commerce; Libraries; Universities; Institutions and private collections was an enjoyable experience.

On the other hand, finding the precise location and angle for the "Now" picture often required extensive investigation. One of the most difficult pictures to research was the classic photo of the first red car to arrive in Santa Monica in 1896. It was like Sam Spade trying to find the Maltese Falcon, digging and digging, until finally the location was pinned down to one of two spots. One was inside a bowling alley and the other was in the parking lot of a gas station, neither of which was very photogenic.

On this picture it was decided to make the contrast between two different modes of transportation in two different eras. Both photos were taken in Santa Monica (nearly a hundred years apart) and both show people arriving in Santa Monica.

Most of the other photographs in this book were taken at the same location as the old photo or as close to it as possible in order to give the proper perspective of a radical change in the scenery.

Speaking of radical changes, it was refreshing to see the flag waving proudly in many of the great old beautiful photographs. At the turn of the century patriotism was in style; Arizona, New Mexico and Oklahoma were still territories and it was fashionable to flaunt one's love of the country.

Without this book ever being shown to a publisher it was decided to self-publish the book, because the values of most publishers are FUBAR*. They crave to accentuate the negative. That is, they would have taken some of the great old beautiful pictures of yesteryear (of which there are many) and then shown how rotten it is today. This book was not made to cure the world's ills, it was made to entertain.

From San Diego to Santa Barbara I discovered a unique phenomenon — the coastline is receding. The ocean is going further away from shore. Either that or the sand is piling up and the beach is extending out into the water. This reminds me of the comedian who yelled, "Don't open the drawbridge; lower the river!"

* FUBAR is the acronym for "Fouled Up Beyond All Recognition."

Richard Henry Dana, Jr. (1815 – 1882) statue at the Dana Point Marina. Author of "Two Years Before the Mast" an expose' on the tough life of the seamen in tall ships.

SANTA BARBARA

The famous "Queen of Missions" was founded in 1786 and services have continued without a break to the present day.

THEN & NOW: Above, Santa Barbara, looking south in 1890. Santa Barbara's famous "Queen of Missions" was founded in 1786 and services have continued without a break to the present day. In 1846 John Charles Fremont raised the U.S. flag at the Presidio and in 1887 the railroad arrived. Below, Santa Barbara today.

THEN & NOW: Above, Santa Barbara's Ledbedder Beach around 1900 and below, today.

THEN & NOW: Above, Santa Barbara in 1900 and below, today.   The horse versus the automobile.   *11*

12

THEN & NOW:
Opposite Page Top — Santa Barbara's "Old Forbush Bath House" around 1890 and below, today.

THEN & NOW:
Above, Summerland (south of Santa Barbara) in 1929, teeming with oil wells. Below, believe it or not, Summerland today. The wells have been moved back and hidden.

THEN & NOW: Above, Santa Barbara's **Ledbedder** Beach is enjoyed by bathers in 1895. Below, today's bathers, left to right are Mark Nelson, Kathy Calhoon, Steve Yoshitake and Patricia Sharples.

THEN & NOW: Above, Santa Barbara's Stearn's Wharf in 1900 was a hustle and bustle of commuters. Below, that same Wharf today in the background has a variety of shops and restaurants.

VENTURA

*In 1782 Father Serra designated Mission San Buenaventura,
meaning "Good Fortune", later shortened to Ventura.*

THEN & NOW: Above, the Ventura Pier around 1900. Below, the same location today. In 1782
Father Junipero Serra named the Mission San Buenaventura after Saint Bonaventure,
a follower of Saint Francis, meaning "Good Fortune", San Buenaventura was later
shortened to Ventura.

THEN & NOW: Above, Ventura in the early part of this century. Below, Ventura today.

THEN & NOW: Above, the Ventura beach around 1900. Below, the same view today. Notice, horses versus autos.

THEN & NOW: Above, Ventura in 1910. Notice the pier in the background. Below, the Ventura Freeway and the same pier today. Ventura is the home of the beautiful Monarch Butterfly which migrates 1000 miles southwest every autumn, returning northward in the spring.

SANTA MONICA

The impressive Pacific Palisades have always been synonymous with Santa Monica.

THEN & NOW: Above, Santa Monica Beach, looking north, around 1910. Below, today. Notice how far the water has receded.

THEN & NOW: Above, Santa Monica bathers in 1910. Below, today. Notice the boy in the center with his hands behind his head is similar in both photos, also the two girls on the right simulating holding their old fashioned bathing suits and the boy standing back and between them and other similarities in these two pictures. This happy group from left to right includes: Lori Coates, Debbie Wandry, Alicia Bower, Johanna Voytis, Kim Delander, Renee Morrell, Paul Bennett, Derek Mair, Sue Ziegler, Jenny Wood, Rick Wilkinson, Jolene Jones, Brian Sutherland, and Alysia Deza.

THEN & NOW:
Above, the Santa Monica Palisades in 2000 B.C. (at the present location of where Wilshire Blvd. ends at the ocean). Below, today. You say they didn't have cameras in 2000 B.C., heh? What about artists? Really, the above picture is around 1880, over a hundred years ago.

THEN & NOW: Above, on April 1, 1896 a historic event took place in Santa Monica. The first electric train arrived. Below, arriving today at the Santa Monica airport are (left to right) Susan Anthony, Stephen Snow, Michael Oliver and Rebecca Baker.

24 *THEN & NOW:* Above, Santa Monica's Pacific Palisades and beach in 1889. Below, today.

THEN & NOW: Above, Santa Monica Beach, looking south toward the Arcadia Hotel and the pier in 1892. Below, today.

THEN & NOW:

Opposite Page Top — The elegant Arcadia Hotel opened in 1887 in Santa Monica and in 1893 newspaper critics reported it to be "the finest hotel on the Pacific coast." It had an elevator, ladies' billiard and reading rooms, a ballroom, a dining room that could seat 200 guests as well as gas and electric lights. Below, today Muscle Beach with its acrobats and volley ball players. Notice how the ocean has receded over the years.

THEN & NOW:

Above, the North Beach Bath House in Santa Monica in 1905 with the Arcadia Hotel in the background. Below, the same location today. The Santa Monica Freeway meets the ocean just behind the two skaters, Cora Adcock and Al Lee.

27

THEN & NOW: Above, Santa Monica Beach, looking north from the cupola of the Arcadia Hotel in 1892. Below, today the size of the beach has changed.

THEN & NOW: Above, the view from the tower of the Arcadia Hotel in 1892. The train and bridge mark the spot where the present Santa Monica Freeway arrives at the ocean. Below, today the freeway runs behind the Holiday Inn building on the right and beneath the street approximately where the bus is located. (The tiny black spots on the top of the 1892 photo are either ballons over the amusement park, printer's ink or as my daughter suggested, fly specks.)

29

THEN & NOW: Above, Santa Monica beach in 1889. Below, today. Who said California's going to drop into the Pacific Ocean? Look at all that beach today!

THEN & NOW: The Pacific Coast Highway north of Santa Monica in 1910. Below, today.

32   *THEN & NOW:* Above, Santa Monica about 1930 where Channel Road meets the beach; notice "Ballantynes" the building in the lower right-hand corner of the photo. Below, the same scene today, "Ballantynes" is now the "Good Food Store."

THEN & NOW: Above, Santa Monica in the roaring twenties, when the Pier was in its heyday. Below, the coast highway has been widened, but the Pier has changed radically except for the cone roofed Merry-Go-Round building.

THEN & NOW:

Above, railroad tracks to Long Wharf in Santa Monica in 1894. The Wharf extended 4,700 feet out over the Pacific Ocean. Santa Monica was a major port until the turn of the century when San Pedro began the new harbor.

THEN & NOW:

Opposite Page Top — Santa Monica in the early twenties. Notice Long Wharf in the distance. Below, today the water has receded. This phenomenon was the same from San Diego to Santa Barbara — the entire Southern California coastline. This seems to refute the gloom and doom forecasters who have been predicting the contrary.

OCEAN PARK

**From classic old Pier Avenue to dazzling
ocean view condominiums.**

THEN & NOW:

Above, Ocean Park around the turn of the
century, looking west at Pier Avenue toward
the ocean. Notice this photo is similar to the
two east facing photos on the following pages
except this photo was apparently taken prior
to the other two photos. Why? Elementary
my dear Watson; see the small balcony railing
above the American flag draped automobile
on the extreme left of the picture? Now, in
the other two photos, looking in the opposite
direction, this small railing is on the right-
hand side of the picture. And in these two
photos (looking east) you can see round white
globed street lights close to this railing. The
above photo was apparently taken prior to
the installation of the street lights. And it
was also probably the Fourth of July as the
flag draped automobile indicates. Below,
today at the same location.

THEN & NOW:

Above, Ocean Park (bordering Venice) about 1905, looking east along Pier Ave. from the ocean front to Main Street in the distance. This classic photograph tells a beautiful story of a time long past. Notice the gentleman in the center of the picture, politely tipping his hat to the lady wearing the long black gloves. She appears to be replying. The shadows also show it is late in the day as the unique two-wheeled baby carriage follows the crowd. Remember this is California; yet with the exception of the little girl in the foreground, every man, woman and child is wearing an elegant hat and they are dressed tastefully and proud. Below, today from the same location; Pier Ave. at this location, is no more, it is now the driveway to a large ocean view condominium complex.

THEN & NOW:

Above, Ocean Park about 1905, looking east along Pier Ave. from the ocean. Notice this photo is similar to the other east facing photo on the previous page only this photo was taken about one hundred feet closer to the ocean (west). Below, today from the same location.

THEN & NOW: Above, the Ocean Park Bath House in 1906 resembled a grand palace for an oriental potentate with heated water, right on the ocean front. Ocean Park was the first development by Abbot Kinney who later began his romantic city the "Venice of America". Ocean Park originally had 200 cottages, stores, a post office and an amusement pier that went 1,250 feet out over the ocean. Below, the grand old Bath House is now gone, replaced by a parking lot. Not very photogenic, right? That is, unless there just happens to be a classic old car there; a two-tone 1929 Nash Four Door Sedan with wooden wheels.

39

VENICE

*Abbot Kinney made his fortune on Sweet Caporal Cigarettes;
he was the father of the "Venice of America."*

THEN & NOW: Above, the Aldebaran Canal in Venice in 1907. Below, the same exact location today. The house behind the first palm tree on the left is the same house above. And the house between the first and second palm tree from the right-hand side is the same as the first house above. What was the Alderbaran Canal is now Market Street.

THEN & NOW: Above, St. Mark's Plaza in Venice in 1906 was a very popular place to promenade. The building on the left is the St. Mark's Hotel on the corner of Windward and the Ocean Front Walk the Bandstand is on the right. Below, today in that exact same location Greg Schwarz and smiling Reggie Bennett stroll hand in hand.

THEN & NOW: Above, "Ding, Ding, Ding went the Trolley." The Pacific Electric Train arrives at the intersection of Windward and Pacific in Venice in 1906. Parasols and fancy hats were in style. Below, today that same intersection.

THEN & NOW: Above, a view of the canals of Venice, California from the lagoon in the early twenties. Venice at that time was the rendezvous for the great motion picture stars of the silent screen — Douglas Fairbanks, Mary Pickford, Rudolph Valentino and Charlie Chaplin to name a few. Harold Lloyd and William S. Hart had cottages by the canals. Norma Shearer, Janet Gaynor and Mae Murray had beach houses nearby. Below, today the lagoon is now the traffic circle at Main Street and Windward Ave. Notice the same two story building on the right-hand side of both pictures.

43

THEN & NOW: Above, the view from the Venice Pier at Windward Avenue in 1906. The Ship Cafe was docked alongside the Pier. The Pier, the ship and even the water are now gone. The sandy beach now extends out into the water at this location. Today, if you were standing at the location of the ship looking toward the beach houses on the right of the old photo you would see a park with Washingtonia fan palm trees and skaters; the Ocean Front Walk is in the background behind the palm trees.

44

THEN & NOW: Above, Venice in the twenties; looking inland from the Ocean Front Walk toward the Lagoon in the distance. These were the glory days of Venice; another attraction, Venice was one of the few "wet" communities in the Southland during Prohibition. Below, today the same street — Windward Avenue.

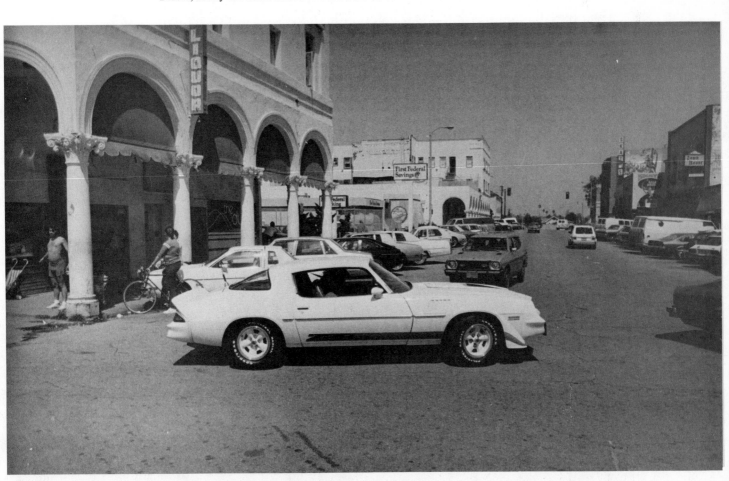

46

THEN & NOW: Above, looking toward the ocean on Windward Avenue in Venice in 1915. The Venice Miniature Railway winds its way down the avenue. Below, today the classic columns are all that is left of Abbott Kinney's wonderful dream.

THEN & NOW: Above, looking toward the ocean from the Venice Lagoon in 1906. In the distance, the Ship Cafe can be seen docked at the Venice Pier. Below, today Windward Avenue has replaced the steps of the promenade and the Lagoon is now a traffic circle. The colonnaded buildings are the last vestige of the great days of Albert Kinney, the father of the "Venice of America," with 16 miles of canals and buildings in the Venetian Renaissance style. Albert Kinney made his fortune with Sweet Caporal Cigarettes. A world traveler, he loved Venice, Italy which is one of the most beautiful cities in the world. The primary reason for the demise of Venice, California's canals was because of an engineering error; there was only one narrow water gate to the sea and proper circulation could not be maintained. In the late twenties most of the canals were filled in and paved as streets.

47

48

THEN & NOW: Above, the Venice Plunge in 1907 on the Ocean Front Walk. The hot salt water pools were a popular attraction. The Plunge is now gone, replaced by a park (below). The location of the Ocean Front Walk is the same place, in the foreground of both pictures.

MARINA DEL REY

*The world's largest man-made
recreational small craft boat harbor.*

THEN & NOW: Above, looking west at the area formerly Lake Los Angeles in the early sixties. Below, Marina del Rey today at Fisherman's Village, Marina del Rey means "Marina of the King."

THEN & NOW: Above, pile driving rig operations in the early sixties. Below, Marina del Rey today. Fisherman's Village is a Cape Cod replica of shops, art galleries and restaurants.

THEN & NOW: Above, an aerial view of Marina del Rey's channel in the early sixties. Below, today Marina del Rey is the world's largest man-made recreational small craft boat harbor with more than 10,000 boats.

THEN & NOW: Above, an aerial view of Marina del Rey looking east in the early sixties. Below, today with the Los Angeles basin in the background.

EL SEGUNDO

A major seaport,
without a dock or wharf.

THEN & NOW: Above, El Segundo in 1911. The future site for Standard Oil Company's refinery. The area selected had to be adjacent to the seacoast where tankers could transport oil to all parts of the world. Because it was Southern California's second oil refinery, they named it El Segundo – "The Second". Six years later – incorporated as a city they christened it "El Segundo a nada" . . . (Second to none). Below, El Segundo today has the lowest tax rate in Southern California because of Standard Oil's location in that city, giving strong support to churches, clubs, schools, Little League, etc.

53

THEN & NOW:

Above, El Segundo's first tanks in 1913. The El Segundo sand dunes were used by numerous Hollywood studios as a replica of the Sahara Desert. Because of Standard Oil's support, El Segundo has one of the finest school systems in the State of California. Below, El Segundo today is a major seaport without a dock or wharf. Underwater lines anchored to buoys, (births) which also have an attached phone line, are pulled up from the ocean floor to the boat. Crude oil arrives from Alaska, Sumatra, Saudi Arabia, South America, etc. Refined products are transported all over the world.

THEN & NOW:

Opposite Page Top — The view is northeast towards Aviation and Imperial Blvds. in El Segundo in the early thirties. Northrop Aircraft moved into the building when it was out in the middle of nowhere, amid uncultivated land inhabited by nothing more than jackrabbits and gophers. And as the Northrop News reported: "Only the wildest dreamer could have foreseen that manufacturing facilities to be built on that 75 acre tract would produce more than 11,000 aircraft in the next 30 years." Below, the heart of the Aerospace Industry — Northrop, Douglas and North American Rockwell have all occupied this site. On the top of the picture is Los Angeles International Airport with Imperial Blvd. running horizontal across the picture. The original Northrop building shown above has been absorbed into the second building from Imperial Blvd. A curved spur of railroad tracks from the intersections can be seen in both pictures.

THEN & NOW: Above, Northrop in El Segundo on March 2, 1938. The caption on this photo was "Boating on Lake Northrop". The picture was taken from Aviation Blvd. looking west at the same building on the previous page. Below, the same location today.

56

THEN & NOW: Above, El Segundo in 1920. The famous red car traveled along the waterfront. The pier where the tankers unloaded is in the background. Below, today the pier is long gone, but the tankers still unload off shore. And today a bike path travels the same route of the old red car through Redondo Beach; Hermosa Beach, Manhattan Beach; El Segundo; Marina del Rey; Venice and Santa Monica.

THEN & NOW: Above, El Segundo in 1920. Below, today a tanker transfers its cargo through underwater lines, while anchored at sea.

MANHATTAN BEACH

A playful seaside community that bears
little resemblance to its namesake.

THEN & NOW: Above, the view north from the Manhattan Beach Pier around 1900. Below, the Strand today.

THEN & NOW:

Above, Manhattan Beach around 1925; looking north toward the Pier. Below, jogging along the Strand in the same place today. Compare the water line in the two pictures. These two photographs appear to resolve the question about the ocean receding – the truth is, notice how the sand is piling up under the pier in the bottom picture.

THEN & NOW:

Opposite Page Top – The view from the Manhattan Beach Pier on July 19, 1925. The trolley ran along the beach from Redondo Beach to downtown Los Angeles. Below, the view along the Strand today with bicyclers and provocatively clad skaters. Notice the dark house with the overhanging roof in the center of both photos still stands today.

HERMOSA BEACH

A fun-loving town, whose name in Spanish means, "Beautiful."

THEN & NOW:

Above, the view south from the Hermosa Beach Pier around 1905. Below, today the view from the pier. The statue of the surfer is Tim Kelly, a fine athlete, lifeguard and surfer who was killed in a tragic automobile accident.

THEN & NOW:

Opposite Page Top — "In olden days a glimpse of stockings was looked on as something shocking," as two bathing beauties (above) pose at the Hermosa Beach Pier in 1905. "Now — Anything Goes" as Denise Vile and Jocelyne Smith pose today (words courtesy of Cole Porter).

THEN & NOW:

Above, Hermosa Beach's "Pier Avenue" looking toward the ocean pier in the early twenties. Below, the exact location today.

THEN & NOW:

Opposite Page Top — Hermosa Beach in 1924 and below, today. Notice the old Hermosa Bitlmore Hotel has disappeared. (Hermosa is Spanish for "Beautiful.")

THEN & NOW: Above, the Hermosa Beach Police in 1918. Below, the Hermosa Beach Police today. Left to Right Officers: Pertruccelli, Koebsell, Bynum, Cavenaugh, Allen, Thompson, Phillips, Whipkey, and Carroll.

THEN & NOW: The Hermosa Beach Fire Department about 1916 and below today: Left to Right: Fritchoff, Geonetta, Aceves, Camant, Engler, and Osekowsky.

THEN & NOW: Above, the "Metropolitan Theatre" in Hermosa Beach in the early twenties with vintage cars parked outside. Below, the same theatre is now two theatres: Cove Cinema No. 1 and No. 2 with surfing movies. Notice the surfer on the corner admiring Kathy Buckman crossing the streeet.

REDONDO BEACH

*What was once upon a time old
Pacific Avenue is now the Pacific Ocean; a well
planned modern Marina and redevelopment project.*

THEN & NOW: Above, multi-masted sailing ships including a five-masted schooner, partially hidden behind the docked steamship, brought lumber to Southern California. The steamers plied the tourist trade. In 1888 the Santa Fe Railway reached Redondo Beach. In 1890 William Hall, a state engineer, discovered a deep water canyon in the ocean floor which led ships right up to the Redondo shore and it became a major seaport until the harbor at San Pedro was developed. Railway freight cars, as well as a windmill, are visible on the pier in this historic 1908 photo. Below, today.

THEN & NOW: Above, is a view from the top of a boxcar far out on Pier No. 1 at the base of Emerald Street in Redondo Beach in 1888. Below, today Pier No. 1 is long gone. The building with the hat shaped roof near the center of the picture sits on the exact spot from where Pier No. 1 started out over the water.

THEN & NOW: Above, the same view as the previous page a couple of years later in 1890. Notice there are more buildings on the hill (Catalina Ave.) and a cupola and flag have been added to the building on the corner of Emerald and Pacific. Also the Casino Building has been built on the beach. As a special note of interest, the building with the flag and cupola or more correctly the corner of Emerald and Pacific is the focal point, the hub or the center of attraction on most of the Redondo Beach photographs. Below, today the building with the hat shaped roof, between the two sailboats is the former location of Pier No. 1. The Redondo horseshoe pier sits to the right of the picture. The building just behind the hat shaped roof is in the exact location of the building with the flag noted above.

71

THEN & NOW: A view of Redondo Beach from Wharf No. 1 at the base of Emerald Street around 1890. Below, the same view today. The building with "The Village" on it is on the exact spot of the building on the corner in the left of the above photo.

72

THEN & NOW: Above, the magnificent Redondo Hotel commanded an excellent view of the beach in this turn of the century photo. The train and hotel are now long gone, replaced by modern condominiums and high-rise apartments. In May 1890, the Redondo Railway ran three trains per day from Los Angeles, 19 miles away. By 1905 electric trains were making 80 round-trips to Los Angeles per day in the fantastic running time of 45 minutes each way — fifty cents one way. To sell real estate at Redondo Beach, promoters would let you ride down and back on the railroad — free — and visit the Redondo Villa Tract. A lot of $90 — $4 down and $4 per month, with no interest or taxes. Below, the white building in the center is the Redondo Library located in Veterans Park the same spot where the Redondo Hotel sat.

THEN & NOW: Above, the view along Pacific Avenue in Redondo Beach around 1910. The first intersection is Pacific and Emerald. Below, what was Pacific Avenue is now the Pacific Ocean.

THEN & NOW: Above, Redondo Beach around 1905. Below, today.

76 *THEN & NOW:* Above, view from Wharf No. 1 located at the base of Emerald Street in Redondo Beach around 1890. Below, today the white library building sits in Veteran's Park, the location of the grand old Redondo Beach Hotel above.

THEN & NOW: Above, the Hotel Redondo, a favorite vacation spot around the turn of the century. Located on land that is now Veterans Park in Redondo Beach, it opened in 1890, prospered but began to decline after 1910. In 1925 the building was sold for $200 as scrap lumber. Below, the Redondo Library in Veterans Park, the former location of the hotel. Jay Holman and Jeff Zotti are doing a wheely through the park.

THEN & NOW: Above, the old Redondo Hotel in the background and the Redondo Railway Company Station in the foreground around 1900. Opposite page, today the Redondo Library is where the Hotel was and the Elk's Club is where the Railway Station was.

THEN & NOW: Opposite page bottom — Redondo Beach at the turn of the century, looking down Pacific Avenue toward Emerald Street, Pier No. 1 is on the right. Below, the same view today. A Marina has been carved out of Pacific Avenue and Pier No. 1 is now the Redondo horseshoe shaped pier with fine restaurants and shops.

THEN & NOW: Above, the Redondo Pier in 1910 offered "A GOOD FISH DINNER FOR 30¢." The street intersection in the distance is the corner of Emerald and Pacific Ave. The Pavillion Building with towers, domes and flags could accommodate 500 dancing couples or seat 4,000 conventioneers. By 1910 Redondo Beach had a population of 2,395. Below, the same location today. Three generations pose to re-enact the scene above (the author's wife, daughter, son-in-law and two grandchildren). The cowboy hat and boots on the boy are the greatest similarity in both pictures; the least are the prices.

80

THEN & NOW: Above, the Redondo Hotel around 1910. Below, the white building under the large tree on the bluff is the Redondo Library which sits in Veterans Park, the same place the hotel was located.

82

THEN & NOW:

Opposite Page Top — A picture postcard of "Redondo Beach, CA — Happy moments" from the twenties. Below, a Redondo Beach resident today: "Melanie Baker."

THEN & NOW:

Above, a picture postcard: "Redondo Beach Bathing Girl about 1910" from John McGehee's collection. Below, a Redondo Beach resident today: "Melanie Baker."

Redondo Beach Cal.   Happy moments.

THEN & NOW: Above, the "Endless Pier", the first of Redondo Beach's horseshoe piers, as seen from just north of the base of Emerald Street in 1917. Two of Redondo's three shipping piers can be seen in the distance. The remains of the third one, destroyed by a storm in 1915, can be seen in the foreground. Below, today Redondo's Pier is a mecca of fine dinner houses and shops.

84

THEN & NOW: Above, bathing beauties at Redondo Beach during the twenties. Below, sexy ladies from the eighties, at the Redondo Village pool: Left to right, Melanie Baker, Nancy Ingles, Heidi Holzinger, Kristie Kreager, Cherylenn Foster and Michelle Bredahl.

THEN & NOW: Above, an aerial view of Redondo Beach around 1920. The magnificent old Redondo Hotel sits in the bottom center of the photo. Opposite page, today the horseshoe pier is one of the few remaining landmarks from those days. Beyond the pier today is the King Harbor Marina which handles over a thousand boats.

THEN & NOW: Opposite page bottom — Redondo Beach around 1920, looking west from the corner of Emerald and Pacific; the building on the left (to the left of **BASE BALL** sign) was the Redondo Plunge. Today the Redondo Seaport Village sits where the Plunge sat. The bottom picture was taken from the exact same location.

THEN & NOW:

Above, the view up Diamond Street from the intersection of Diamond & Pacific Ave. in Redondo Beach during the early twenties. The El Ja Hotel at the right is said to have been frequented by Charlie Chaplin. Below, today Pacific Ave. is a dock for plush yachts and the El Ja Hotel is the ocean view condominium on the right-hand side of the picture.

Opposite Page Top — The Bank Building with the clock was on the corner of Pacific and Emerald in Redondo Beach. The gasoline age of the early twenties emerged, as the number of automobiles indicate. This intersection no longer exists; a modern ocean view condominium on the extreme right-hand side sits on the exact spot of Bank Building above. The lower walk (adjacent to the water) is called "The International Boardwalk" — a group of unique shops representing Mexico, Africa, Japan, Italy, China, Indonesia and America. There is also whale watching and harbor cruises, a boat hoist and an amusement center.

THEN & NOW: The Redondo Beach salt-water plunge above around 1910. The Plunge featured warm and cold salt-water and could accommodate 2000 bathers. Below, today the Redondo Seaport Village is located on the same spot. The Seaport Village is a modern replica of a New England Seaport with fine restaurants and shops.

THEN & NOW: Above, the Redondo Hot Salt Water Plunge was a massive 1909 structure, 278 by 156 feet — it held three pools. There was a baby pool 30 by 70 feet; a high diving pool 30 by 70 feet with water 9 feet deep and a main pool 70 by 157 feet, with water three to five feet in depth. All of the pools were supplied with a continuous flow of warm salt water from the electric power plant. The Plunge also had 1,350 dressing rooms. This photo taken in the twenties was apparently on the Fourth of July by the looks of the proud display of 'Old Glory' from the walls and ceiling. Below, the same spot today — the Redondo Seaport Village.

THEN & NOW: Above, an aerial view of the Redondo Beach pier area around 1940. Below, today Torrance Blvd. comes clear to the beach where it circles. Notice the white church steeple on Torrance Blvd. is visible in both photographs. Just behind the Pier the Redondo Seaport Village sits on top of the massive parking structure and just behind Seaport Village the Redondo Village Condominium completes the modern Redevelopment Program.

PALOS VERDES

*Beautiful white homes, with red tile
roofs and spectacular views of the Pacific; on a
clear day you can see forever.*

THEN & NOW:

Above, the view northward from above the Malaga Cove Plaza in Palos Verdes Estates in 1928. At this time the drugstore building stood alone in the Plaza. On October 8, 1542 on his first sight of this bay Juan Rodriguez Cabrillo, the Spanish explorer prophetically named it, "La Bahia de los Fumas," (Bay of Smokes). Historians report that the Indians were having a rabbit hunt and had set fire to the underbrush to smoke out their prey. Even today, October is a unique month at the beach because of its lack of sea breeze and the Los Angeles basin smog drifts out over the water, trapped by an inversion layer of warm air lying above the basin; the rest of the year the ocean breeze sweeps the shoreline clean. Below, today Neptune's Fountain can be seen to the right of the drugstore building.

THEN & NOW: Above, the dedication of Neptune's fountain in the Malaga Cove Plaza in Palos Verdes in 1930. Below, today.

THEN & NOW: Palos Verdes in 1927 above and today below. Around 40 years ago a famous MGM photograher advised me, "Palos Verdes is the coming thing; you should try and get some property there." But 40 years ago when I was a young man I wanted a new car. I wish I would have taken Mr. Rosson's advice.

95

THEN & NOW:

Opposite Page Top — Palos Verdes Estates around 1910. The first building of the Malaga Cove Plaza Shopping Center can be seen in the distance. Above, today the author's daughter, Nancy, poses at the exact same location.

Opposite Page Center — Palos Verdes around 1920, below today. Marineland sits to the right of the picture. Whales leap 18 feet out of the water to take a fish from the mouth of a trainer; Sea Lions sing tunes and Dolphins jump in spectacular acrobatics.

THEN & NOW: Above, Palos Verdes around 1925. The view toward the Malaga Cove Plaza (looking north). Below, the same spot today.

THEN & NOW: Above, view from Palos Verdes toward Redondo Beach in 1928. The Haggarty mansion at the left (with the cupola) sits along the cliff. Below, today (that mansion became the neighborhood church.)

THEN & NOW:

Above, looking southwest toward the Malaga Cove Plaza in Palos Verdes around 1925. Below, today.

Opposite Page Top — A view of the Malaga Cove and Montemalaga areas of Palos Verdes Estates from the air in January 1927. Below, today.

THEN & NOW:

Above, Portuguese Bend in Palos Verdes in 1940 as seen in a northwesterly direction. Below, today.

SAN PEDRO

*Cruise ships sail for exotic places
all over the Atlantic and Pacific and around the world.*

THEN & NOW:

Above, San Pedro in 1908. The locomotive is pushing rocks out to form the harbor breakwater. Below, the same railroad today, with the author's wife June.

THEN & NOW:

Above, San Pedro Harbor in 1908. Notice the U.S. Navy Battle Fleet in the distance. Teddy Roosevelt's Great White Fleet is on parade inside the new breakwater. Below, Ports O'Call Village today, a portion of which is a replica of an old New England seacoast village.

104

THEN & NOW:

OPPOSITE PAGE ABOVE: The title of this historic painting by the famous marine artist Duncan Gleason is "Cabrillo Discovering Los Angeles Harbor in 1542." This authentic painting hangs in the Los Angeles Maritime Museum and is through the courtesy of the Los Angeles Harbor Department. Below, Captain John Cox stands on the bridge of the cruise ship "Azure Seas" as it heads toward the Vincent Thomas Bridge looming in the background. The "Azure Seas" had just finished sailing the exact route that Cabrillo did, up the Mexican coast to the Los Angeles Harbor.

105

Above, west coast windjammers off San Pedro at the turn of the century. Below, the exact same location today; notice the breakwater in the left background. This photo was taken from the bridge of the cruise ship "Azure Seas" as she was being guided through the Los Angeles Harbor by San Pedro Harbor Pilot Patrick Donohugh, toward San Pedro's main channel. The Palos Verdes Peninsula can also be seen in the distance. The Los Angeles Harbor was started in 1889 — today it is protected by a 9-mile breakwater. The combined Port of Long Beach and Port of Los Angeles make up the largest manmade harbor in the world with islands and channels that make up 50 miles of waterfront.

OPPOSITE PAGE TOP: The four-masted schooner "Manila" in San Pedro in the late 90's, unloading lumber. The "Manila" was sunk on July 8, 1917 in the Central Pacific, near the equator during World War I by Count Felix Von Luckner. In Lowell Thomas' fascinating book, "The Sea Devil," he described how Von Luckner sunk fourteen ships in the Atlantic and Pacific, "without ever having taken a human life . . . " The book reads like an Errol Flynn movie. Von Luckner's raider was a former American Clipper Ship. Below, the "Love Boat" (the "Pacific Princess.) Behind it, the "Princess Louise" an old steamer converted into a plush floating restaurant by the Vincent Thomas Bridge.

PACIFIC PRINCESS

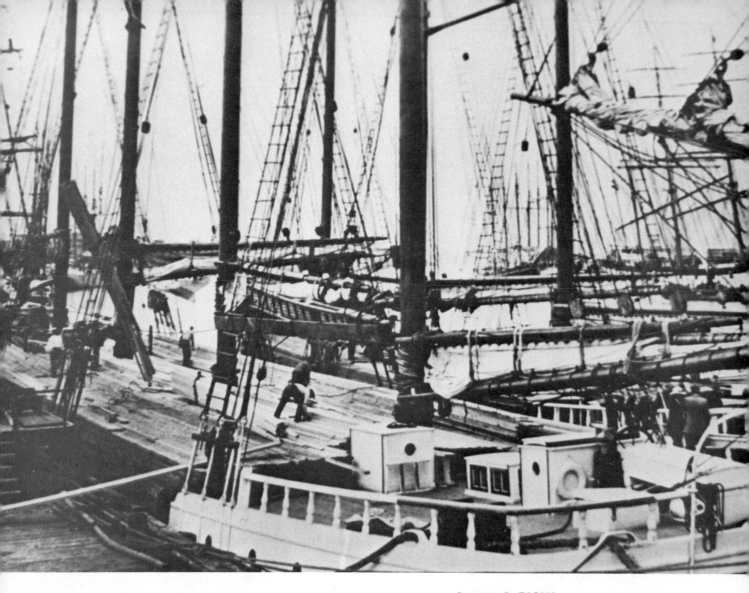

THEN & NOW:

Above, a schooner unloading lumber in San Pedro in the latter part of the last century. Below, the modern technology of containerization has quintupled productivity. The three huge cranes are container loaders; the cranes are loading the "Manukai."

108

THEN & NOW:

OPPOSITE PAGE TOP: Typical of the tall ships of the 1890's that sailed the Pacific is the "Sea Witch" painted by Duncan Gleason and hanging in the Los Angeles Maritime Museum. (The picture of the "Sea Witch" is through the courtesy of Duncan Gleason and the Los Angeles Maritime Museum.) Below, the freighter "Star World" loads up at San Pedro.

THEN & NOW:

After sailing from San Pedro, the "Hermosa" arrives at Avalon, on Catalina Island (above) in 1905. Below, Catalina today.

THEN & NOW:

OPPOSITE PAGE TOP: The "Cabrillo" loads up for Catalina in 1905 in east San Pedro. Below, the "Azure Seas" loads up for Mexico today.

112

THEN & NOW:

Above, the coastal passenger steamer "Santa Rosa" enters San Pedro's main channel in 1910. The schooner in the foreground is the "A.J. West" and to the right the "Alert" and the "Formosa" (three west coast windjammers). The "Santa Rosa" was wrecked at Point Arguillo in 1911. Notice the resemblance to Laurel and Hardy exiting stage right. Below, the freighter "Duke Star" loads up at San Pedro. Notice the huge multimillion dollar crane (a container loader) next to the "Duke Star."

OPPOSITE PAGE TOP: San Pedro, looking southeast toward Dead Man's Island at Los Angeles Harbor around the turn of the century. Below, the "Royal Viking Sky" cruise ship enters the Los Angeles Harbor. The Viking Ships are magnificent cruise ships that are actually floating pleasure palaces, that travel both the Atlantic and Pacific Oceans.

THEN & NOW: Above, the Port of Los Angeles in 1900. A three masted schooner is helped into San Pedro's main channel by a sturdy tug boat. The schooners were used primarily to haul lumber into growing Southern California. Below, the super-freighter President Hoover is aided by a tug boat in that same channel framed by the massive Vincent Thomas Bridge.

THEN & NOW: Above, Windjammers from left to right the "A.J. West", the "Alert" and the "Formosa" unload lumber from the northwest in east San Pedro around 1910. Ships also carried machinery, kerosene, and even ice to California, clear around the bottom of South America (the horn). They brought back sugar, rice, tea, silk and coal, as well as passengers. The schooner "Alert" above was lost in the Tongas in 1923, the crew of eight reached shore safely. Below, the "Duke Star" unloads in San Pedro's main channel. The three giant cranes to the right can load and unload containers in 20% of the time it took longshoremen to transfer individual packages of cargo. The technology of containerization has revolutionized the shipping industry.

115

117

THEN & NOW:

Above, the "Sea Witch" painted by Duncan Gleason and hanging in the Los Angeles Maritime Museum was typical of Clipper Ships frequently seen on the North American west coast in the last century. (The picture of the "Sea Witch" is through the courtesy of Duncan Gleason and the Los Angeles Maritime Museum). Below, a present day cargo vessel exits San Pedro's main channel, passing Ports O'Call Village on the left.

Opposite Page Top — San Pedro's main channel around the turn of the century. Lumber from the Northwest for the burgeonning Los Angeles sits on the dock. Below, today the formidable Vincent Thomas Bridge soars 185 feet over this same channel connecting San Pedro with Terminal Island. This harbor is the point of departure for cruises to Mexico, Hawaii, the far east and the around the world.

THEN & NOW: Above, the "Ocean King" especially painted and presented to the Los Angeles Maritime Museum by the noted marine artist of Carmel, Hans Skaalagard. Built in Maine in 1874, the King was lost off the Oregon coast in 1887. All hands were saved by the sealing schooner "Angel Dolly." (The picture of the "Ocean King" is through the courtesy of Hans Skaalagard and the Los Angeles Maritime Museum.) Below, the "Love Boat" (the "Pacific Princess") and next to her is an authentic side wheeler paddle boat with a plush cocktail lounge and restaurant. Built in 1924 the "Princess" holds 148 passengers. It was the original glass bottom boat at Catalina built by the Wrigley Co.

118

THEN & NOW: Above, around the turn of the century the "Hermosa" leaving San Pedro with fun-seekers. Hats, ties and jackets were in style. Below, today the "Azure Seas" leaving San Pedro with casual funseekers for a weekend cruise to Mexico. Remember when — the rule was — jacket and ties required — now it's — no bare feet allowed.

THEN & NOW: Above, the "Cabrillo" the Catalina Boat. Launched in 1904 at Wilmington, she carried passengers between San Pedro and Avalon. Below, the "Pacific Princess — the famous star of the "Love Boat" TV show is a British registered cruise ship that sails from San Pedro to the Mexican Riviera (Acapulco, Puerto Vallarta, etc.). It features musical revues, dancing, deck sports, swimming, a casino, theatre, etc.

THEN & NOW: One of the few tall ships still active, the "Christian Radich" shown here birthed at the Los Angeles Maritime Museum in San Pedro. She is probably best remembered for the starring role in "Windjammer" an early wide screen spectacular in 1957. Below, in contrast to the sailing ship, the "Duke Star" today.

THEN & NOW: Above, at San Pedro's "Ports O'Call" the Buccaneer Queen manuevers at the dock. This 100 foot Square Rigged Barque is similar to early ships that sailed in the 1800's. They were used as Slavers, for Cod fishing and Coastal Traders. A plush cocktail bar below decks seats 62 people. It is continually in use for harbor cruisers; party cruises at sea, whale watching (in the winter) and trips to Avalon Bay at Catalina Island. Below, the Pacific Princess.

THEN & NOW:

Opposite Page Top — At San Pedro's "Ports O'Call" the Buccaneer Queen sails the main channel. Below, the "Austral Rainbow" a modern containerized cargo ship exits that same channel.

LONG BEACH

*From a sleepy western town
to the largest man-made harbor in the world;
the present home of the majestic "Queen Mary."*

THEN & NOW:

The Long Beach Hotel, which burned down in 1888. Below, the same location today.

THEN & NOW:

Opposite Page Top — Pine Ave. Pier in Long Beach in 1893. The sign on the entrance to the pier says: "Bicycle riders are warned not to ride machines on the sidewalks or wharf or discharge firearms on the wharf or within the City Limits PENALTY (not legible)." Below, the same location today during the Grand Prix. The line of palm trees in the center of the road sit where the Pier was once located.

125

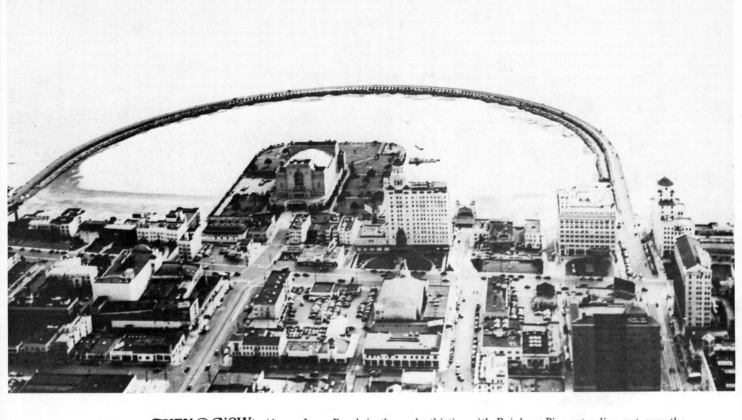

THEN & NOW: Above, Long Beach in the early thirties with Rainbow Pier extending out over the Pacific Ocean. Below, today part of the man-made massive Port of Long Beach now sits out in the ocean, a home for the majestic Queen Mary. Notice the small island to the left of the photo, the oil wells have been disguised as high-rise buildings.

THEN & NOW: Above, the Magnolia Ave. Pier in Long Beach in 1890 runs out into the Pacific Ocean. Below today, the same ocean has been converted into the Port of Long Beach and the Port of Los Angeles, sharing the world's largest man-made harbor. Channels and islands covering 50 miles of developed waterfront, protected by a 9 mile breakwater. The causeway running horizontally across the picture, from the striped high-rise, sits on the exact location of the old Magnolia Ave. Pier.

127

THEN & NOW:

Above, Long Beach 1920. The Virginia Hotel to the left. The white building to the right is the Long Beach Bath House. Below, high-rise office buildings dominate the same locations. Notice how the water has receded.

THEN & NOW:

Opposite Page Top – Long Beach in 1897 at Pine Avenue and 2nd Street. Below, today.

130

THEN & NOW:

Opposite Page Top — Pine Ave. Pier in Long Beach in 1897 with the original pavillion. Below, the same location today during the Grand Prix. In the background the retired Cunard Liner "Queen Mary" still reigns in Long Beach harbor.

THEN & NOW:

Above, Long Beach, 1912. Looking toward shore from Pine Ave. Pier. Automobiles were beginning to take the place of horses. Below, the exact location today; the only thing recognizable is the Bank of America Building with its clock tower in the background.

THEN & NOW:

Above, Pine Ave. Pier in Long Beach in 1901. True horse power was in style. Below, the row of palm trees to the right of the picture are on the location of the Pier, while the "Queen Mary" is moored on the left of the photo.

THEN & NOW:

Opposite Page Top – Long Beach, 1889. Looking south from the Pine Avenue Pier Pavillion. Below, the same location today during the Grand Prix.

THEN & NOW: Above, the "Harvard" (about 1915) leaves the entrance to the Los Angeles Harbor at Angels Gate. The "Harvard" and its twin sister the "Yale" were plush passenger vessels that made an overnight trip to San Francisco, often to see football games. The "Harvard" went on the rocks at Point Arguello on May 30, 1931. Below, the "Queen Mary" floats proudly in what once was the open sea of the Pacific Ocean, but is now the Port of Los Angeles and the Port of Long Beach, the largest man-made harbor in the world, shielded by a 9 mile breakwater. The stately "Queen Mary" is still a pleasure palace and it is open for tours, dining, or you can sleep on board in staterooms run as a hotel.

THEN & NOW: Above, the "Yale" the sister ship to the "Harvard" (opposite page) entering Los Angeles Harbor about 1921. Below, the huge "Queen Mary." After a 14,500 mile journey clear down under Cape Horn at the bottom of the world in 1967 the "Queen Mary" docked at its Long Beach home.

THEN & NOW: Above, the battleship "New Jersey" being refurbished at the Long Beach Navy Yard. The "New Jersey" sunk the light Japanese cruiser "Katori" and destroyer "Maikaze" at Eniwetok Atoll in World War II. In the Luzon campaign, Admiral Halsey commanded the Fleet from the "New Jersey." She also saw action in Viet Nam. OPPOSITE PAGE TOP: The "Constitution" painted by Duncan Gleason hangs in the Los Angeles Maritime Museum; she was over 200 feet long and carried 55 heavy guns. The "Constitution" was in Los Angeles in 1933, where she attracted the largest crowd ever to visit her. In 1804 the "Constitution" took part in five attacks on Tripoli in North Africa. In the War of 1812 she destroyed the British frigate "Guerriere." Because British shot bounced off her tough hull during this battle the sailors nicknamed her "Old Ironsides." She also sank the British warship "Java." Oliver Wendell Holmes made her immortal with his poem "Old Ironsides." (The picture of the "Constitution" is through the courtesy of Duncan Gleason and the Los Angeles Maritime Museum.) OPPOSITE PAGE BOTTOM: Another view of the illustrious "New Jersey" at the Long Beach Navy Yard.

THEN & NOW: Above, another magnificent view of the "Constitution" courtesy of Duncan Gleason and the Los Angeles Maritime Museum. Below, the "New Jersey" (58,000 tons with a speed of 35 knots) at the Long Beach Navy Yard.

NEWPORT

The Gold Coast — magnificent waterfront homes,
with a yacht moored at nearly every door.

THEN & NOW:

Above, Newport Beach, Balboa Harbor entrance on April 12, 1928 on an exceptionally clear day. Below, today the Gold Coast with magnificent waterfront homes and yachts. In the 1940's the Balboa Pavillion sent the Big Band sounds across the nation and gave birth to a dance — The Balboa Hop.

140 *THEN & NOW:* Above, Newport Beach in 1918. Looking west along Bay Avenue from Main Street. The old fire station is on the left. Below, today everything has changed except the old house on the corner (hidden by the tree), it looked the same.

LAGUNA

A French Riviera setting; long known as an
art colony, the Pageant of Living Masters has local residents
don costumes and become living pictures.

THEN & NOW: Above, Laguna Beach around 1915. Below, Laguna today with its French Riviera setting has been long known as an art colony. Laguna is famous for its Festival of Arts and Pageant of Living Masters in which the local residents don costumes and become living pictures. The show is so professional that it is difficult to believe that these pictures are really alive. All the great painting of the masters are recreated and the show now attracts 300,000 spectators annually.

141

THEN & NOW: Above, Laguna Beach around 1910.   Below, today at the exact same location.

THEN & NOW: Above, Laguna Beach near the turn of the century. Below, bikini clad bathers enjoy Laguna's fine beach. Standing in front of the lifeboat. Left to Right: Karen Lee Gilbert (holding baby), Brenda Condon, Craig Condon, Annie Winding, Benni T. Winding.

143

144

THEN & NOW:

Opposite Page Top — Seal Rock at Laguna Beach around 1910. Above bathers enjoy the same beach. Left to right: Dennis Harper, Susan Harper, Susan Wildenberg, Donna Gersten and Craig Harper.

THEN & NOW:

Opposite Page Bottom — Pacific Coast Highway in Laguna Beach in 1927 and below, today. Notice the "White House" is the same location in both photographs.

THEN & NOW: Above, Pacific Coast Highway in Laguna Beach in 1927 and below, today.

THEN & NOW: Above, Laguna Beach in the early twenties. Looking east on Forest Avenue from the Pacific Coast Highway. Below today, sixty years later. Notice the Drug Store in the same location.

THEN & NOW: Above, the Laguna Beach Hotel in the early part of the century. Below, today.

THEN & NOW: Above, Laguna Beach around 1915. The intersection of Forest Ave. and Third Street is on the right-hand side of the picture. Below, today the City Hall sits on that corner (where the flag is waving).

THEN & NOW:

Above, Laguna Beach in the early thirties.
Opposite Page Top — today.

THEN & NOW:

Below, Laguna Beach in 1927. Opposite
Page Bottom — today at the same location.

LA JOLLA

**A stretch of picturesque seacoast
in a tradition of Meditteranean splendor.**

THEN & NOW: Above, La Jolla in 1910, Scripps Institution of Oceanography can be seen near the center of the picture. Below, La Jolla today.

THEN & NOW: Above, La Jolla in 1910. The first building of the Scripps Institution of Oceanography. Below, today the roof of that same building can be seen, surrounded by newer buildings. Just north of San Diego, La Jolla is a 5 mile stretch of Mediterranean California at its most enchanting. The hills and steep cliffs along the beautiful beaches present magnificent views of the ocean to observe pelicans and seagulls diving for fish.

153

THEN & NOW: Above, La Jolla in 1910. The first building of the Scripps Institution of Oceanography. Below, today the second story of that building can be seen near the center of the photo. Scripps is now part of the University of California at San Diego and it is world renowned as a center for research of the mysteries of the sea.

154

THEN & NOW: Above, La Jolla in 1000 BC (Would you believe 1907?) Below, today the same location; buildings of the Scripps Institution of Oceanography.

THEN & NOW: Above, La Jolla in 1910. The first building of the Scripps Institution of Oceanography. Below, today trees surround the exact location. Notice how the water has receded.

SAN DIEGO

Discovered by Juan Rodriguez Cabrillo in 1542;
one of the great natural harbors of the world.

THEN & NOW: Above, tall masted sailing ships in San Diego Bay in the 1880's. Below, U.S. Navy ships today in San Diego Bay. Juan Rodriguez Cabrillo arrived in San Diego in 1542. The West Coast's first settlement was not developed until 1769 when Father Junipero Serra started the Mission San Diego de Alcola on Presidio Hill. This is still a beautiful tourist attraction today.

THEN & NOW: Above, San Diego Bay in 1890. The steamer "City of Topeka" is surrounded by tall sailing ships. Below, today the U.S. Navy in San Diego Bay. San Diego Harbor is huge, almost landlocked and it is one of the world's best deepwater ports. San Diego is an excellent all-year vacation city, with an average 70°F temperature with low humidity. While we took the tour around the great harbor, jet fighters would streak around the sky, then they would hover above the flat-top behind the destroyer below. Smooth, precision vertical landing and take-offs were practiced. A far cry from Eugene Ely's 1911 San Diego flight.

THEN & NOW: Above, the British Sailing Ship "Toxteth" enters the San Diego harbor in the early part of the century. The "Toxteth" was made of iron; she was reported as missing in the vicinity of Cape Horn in 1908. Below, the aircraft carrier "Coral Sea" dwarfs a sailboat. The "Coral Sea" is 979 feet long (three football fields with 79 feet left over) with a crew of 4,000. It can carry 70 aircraft.

THEN & NOW: Above, the Cliff House in Ocean Beach in 1892. Below, the same location today.

THEN & NOW: Above, a San Diego wharf in 1895 when clipper ships dominated the seas. Discovered in 1542 by Juan Rodriguez Cabrillo, San Diego Bay is one of the great natural harbors of the world. Below, U.S. Navy destroyers line the dock.

THEN & NOW: Above, Ocean Beach (adjacent to San Diego) in 1913. Notice, there were a few daredevils in bathing suits. Below, the exact same spot today.

THEN & NOW: Above, San Diego in 1911. The Aviator Eugene Ely flying off the deck of the "Pennsylvania". Notice the sailors crowded on the deck of a submarine in the background watching this historic event. Below, the modern aircraft carrier today in San Diego harbor.

THEN & NOW:

Above, in San Diego Bay in 1908; men of the "USS Louisiana" pose proudly on their battle wagon. Below, a sailing sloop looks like a toy by the aircraft carrier "Coral Sea" in San Diego Bay.

THEN & NOW:

Opposite Page Top – Mission Bay as seen from Old Town in San Diego in 1898. Below, Mission Bay today, with "Sea World" in the foreground where Killer Whales do acrobatics. There are sharks; dolphins; pearl diving; an underwater show; a seal and otter show; antarctic penguins; exotic birds and much more.

ETCETERA

A potpourri of American Heritage, Ships
People, Places and Icebergs.

THEN & NOW: Above, left — Marina del Rey's statue of a seaman. Right — Marina del Rey's reproduction of a New England Cape Cod Lighthouse.

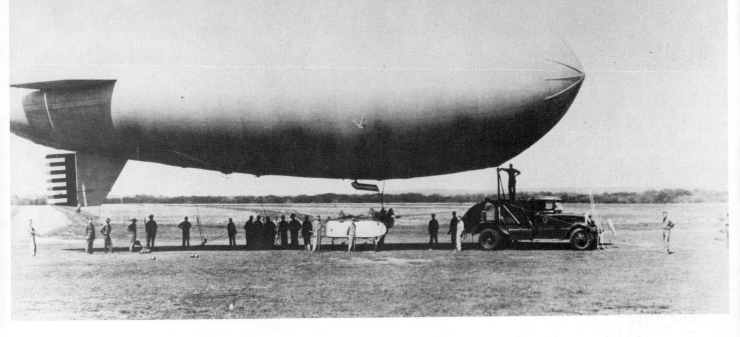

THEN & NOW: The above picture shows a Blimp from the early part of this century. Notice the basket hanging precariously by wires under this old airship. Below, today the Goodyear Blimp "Columbia" at its base at Gardena, California. In the foreground, L to R Corky Belanger (the pilot), George Morris and Melanie Baker. Most of the "NOW" aerial shots of the Southern California seacoast in this book were taken from the "Columbia"; it makes an excellent camera platform and is continually in demand by motion picture and TV cameramen. The dotted lines on the underside of the "Columbia" are actually small colored lights that have been computerized to flash animated designs and messages out of the Southern California evening sky.

THEN & NOW: Above, Catalina Island's world famous landmark, the Casino Ballroom, the home of the Big Bands of yesteryear and today. Below, Catalina's picturesque Avalon Bay (see page 110 for the olden days). Catalina is a real fun island. Glass bottom boats are an attraction, especially when divers swim among the many colored fish. There is also camping, horseback riding, fishing, boating, diving and scenic drives.

THEN & NOW: One of the true beauty spots of Southern California's seacoast that looks the same then and now is Laguna's Seal Rock above, painted by the author, below.

170

THEN & NOW:

An aerial view of Redondo Beach's King Harbor Marina (the picture of this area before the Marina can be seen on page 86). In 1890 William Hall, a state engineer discovered a deep underwater canyon at Redondo Beach which led ships right up to the Redondo shore and it became a major seaport until the harbor at San Pedro was developed. Would you believe a serious study has been made to bring Antarctic icebergs to Southern California? Why would anyone want to bring icebergs clear from the South Pole? Because — "The world's total water resources are estimated to be 97 percent sea water and only 3 percent fresh water. Three-fourths of the fresh water is held in the form of ice, most of it (about 90 percent) in the Antarctic." — as a report by the Rand Corporation prepared for the National Science Foundation acknowledges.

We asked John L. Hult of the Engineering Sciences Department of Rand, who helped prepare the report, about the use of the Redondo deep submarine canyon as a location to bring the Antarctic icebergs.

Mr. Hult admitted, "It is premature to describe how or if the Redondo Trench might be used as an iceberg terminal. It does offer attractive deep water and nearby electric generating stations could benefit from cooling water. However, there are many factors that must be considered, including environmental impact and public reaction."

He advised, "The greatest demand for large quantities of fresh water are most likely to develop for augmentation of the Colorado and for irrigation of coastal plains. However, Redondo may still be an attractive terminal for quantities of about a million acre feet per year."

We were surprised to learn of the futuristic plans to tow iceberg trains 50 miles long with atomic tugs. The ten month journey at 1 knot would require special plastic "quilts", designed to restrict melting to 10 percent of the iceberg's weight. In addition to the atomic tugs, there would be a variety of auxiliary launches, helicopters and other equipment.

At their terminal the icebergs would be chopped into 10 foot chunks and fed into a storage plant. Amazingly, the cost per acre-foot of water would be less than half the cost of California aqueduct water. And the iceberg water would be appreciably purer than the aqueduct water.

The concept of towing icebergs is not a new idea. At the turn of the century, Antarctic icebergs were transported by steamship to arid Callao, Peru — practically on the equator.

THEN & NOW: Above, at Ports O'Call Village in San Pedro, the "Estella" built in the late eighteen hundreds was often used for smuggling (narcotics and other contraband). The past owners are now getting free room and board in the Federal Prison. Below from the left, the "Estella," the "Showboat" (a stern wheel paddle boat, a replica of the famed Mississippi River Boats) and the "Princess" (a side wheeler paddle boat — see page 118).

THEN & NOW: Above, La Jolla's beautiful beach today. The Scripps Institute Pier can be seen in the distance (see page 152 for how it looked in 1910). Below, Cabrillo Beach in the Los Angeles Harbor (see page 105 for Cabrillo's first sight of this beach).

THEN & NOW: Above, San Diego's Embarcadero includes fine waterfront dining, nautical gift shops and the former square-rigger "Star of India," the oldest (1863) iron-hulled sailing ship still afloat. This magnificent old ship is part of a Maritime Museum Fleet moored along the Embarcedero which includes the ferryboat "Berkeley" from San Francisco and the yacht "Medea". There are also long-range tuna boats (that have their own helicopters and small chase boats) that travel as far as off the coast of Africa to catch tuna. (See photo below.)

173

THEN & NOW: Above, the "Royal Viking Sky" cruise ship sails up San Pedro's main channel. Below, from the bridge of the cruise ship "Azure Seas," Captain John Cox and Staff Captain Dimitrios Mylonis observe Ports O'Call Village in San Pedro (see page 111 for old timers party trips).

INDEX